Haiku Pop

A collection of Pop Culture Haiku

By: Fritz Schaper

This book is dedicated to my brother George Louis Killenger Fitzgerald III -- who told always told me

"When they say you can't – show them how you did"

Chapter 1
Star Wars

Star Wars was ruined
When I found out Stormtroopers
Were child soldiers

Turns out Darth Vader
Was a bitch under that mask
Until James Earl Jones

Sand People may hide
Their numbers but they never
Hide their emotions

Wish I was Lando
But I can not rock a cape
Except that I can

Boba Fett did shit
He went out like a punk ass
Didn't kill one guy

Kenobi did not
Go back to free Annie's Mom
No reason not to

They left Chewie Out
When they gave out the medals
Real space racism

Kylo wear a shirt
No one wants to see your nips
Cover yourself please

Leia Organa
Our favorite space princess
Sweet sticky bun hair

Turns out Last Jedi
Sucks harder than a porn star
Trying a come back

Chapter 2
He-Man and the Masters of the Universe

He Man sweet He Man
Why won't you let me inside
Your heart or Greyskull?

Mauve fur bikini
What sweet secret do you hold
The sword of He Man?

Please listen Beast Man
The bidet is full of hair
And it is orange

Your fur bikini
So tight so maroon and hot
Leave it on my floor

Question Prince Adam
And his bizarre fashion sense
Medieval doorman

The heroes journey
Is fun riding a tiger
That will not bite you

Here's one Man At Arms
Why do your cars not have wheels
They work better round

Wait Man E Faces
A total of 3 faces
Is not that Man E

Stinkor could not find
A roommate or place to live
Gee I wonder why

Merman use the tub
I had it installed for you
Lockjaw would just rust

Why do I share home
With a gang of foul henchmen
Snake Mountain has space

I have no eye balls
I have no eye lids or nose
I have no senses

I once caught He Man
In the bathroom of club smash
But he got away

There are zero dogs
On Eternia of course
They have giant cats

The He Man Theme Song
Is the greatest song ever
Skeletor is sad

Chapter 3
Back To The Future

Marty did not know
His family when he came
Back to the future

Doc knew Marty how
This friendship makes no damn sense
Marty is no nerd

Biff back in high school
Grabbed at my wife in a car
Now he waxes mine

You have a machine
That lets you do time travel
Why are you worried

How did you not see
The weird kid grabbing his crotch
At the end of 3

Chapter 4
The Simpsons

We all know Homer
Is secretly our own dad
That's why we love him

Inept sideshow Bob
Farewell elaborate schemes
Hello Mr Firearm

Lisa plays the sax
Which is a weird instrument
For a little girl

Tried an Apu one
But his last name is too long
Even for line 2

Skinner the legend
Is he Norman Bates maybe
I don't want to know

Speaking of Seymour
Let us not forget steamed hams
Nay Impossible

Springfield is the place
Wiggum would never catch you
Rip the mattress tag

Chapter 5
Friends (The 90's Sitcom)

Question for the friends
New York is huge why don't you
Know any non white folks

Joey how can you
Afford that place in New York
Are you a male whore

No way Ross would score
With chicks of that caliber
Unless he was rich

Monica will cheat
Every chance she gets to cheat
Just like my ex wife

It is a known fact
That Phoebe Buffay was once
A street criminal

Chapter 6
Seinfeld

Kramer is racist
Elaine is a piece of ass
George and Jerry meh

Now ask yourself this
Back in the 1990s
Were you sponge worthy

Seinfeld was a jerk
Sometimes life imitates art
He is still a jerk

Oh yes they were real
And yes they were fantastic
Now that ship has sailed

You must not forget
The Moops invaded Europe
Costanza still lost

Chapter 7
Gilligan's Island

Who said the island
Belongs just to Gilligan
I vote for Ginger

Fix the boat loser
No coconut radio
We need to escape

If I were skipper
The redhead would be my girl
The rest can all starve

How the Globetrotters
Found a way off the island
I will never know

Good thing that no one
Had coconut allergies
Or they would be dead

Chapter 8
The Smurfs

The Smurfs are hippies
They all live in a commune
And no one wears shoes

The Snorks are lousy
A clear rip off of the Smurfs
Fuck you lousy Snorks

Papa Smurf is mad
For power and revenge
Against Grandpa Smurf

There is just 1 girl
I expect she will #metoo
Odds are in favor

One terrorist Smurf
Jokey Smurf gave bombs as gifts
That's horrific

Chapter 9
G.I. Joe

Cobra Commander
Never could beat GI Joe
He must beat himself

GI Joe is lame
Knowing is half the battle
One they will not win

Destro the leader
At least his helmet is cool
But not the necklace

Zartan change color
Quick to camouflage yourself
Stupid Joe won't know

I just have to say
That the name Sergeant Slaughter
Is not kid friendly

Chapter 10
The Jetsons

Question for Jetsons
Why treadmills on the outside
That's needless danger

Poor sad George Jetson
His wife takes all his money
His kids are selfish

Dude Astro can talk
That's either the coolest thing
Or the least cool thing

Chapter 11
Harry Potter

Harry how is it
That you still can't figure out
It is Voldemort

Gingers make the best friends
Ron Weasley proves that each page
Of the full story

If you have magic
You don't ever need a job
You have magic fool

Why does Hermione
Waste her time with those 2 dorks
She is the best witch

I love Dumbledore
Turns out he might love me back
But not the same way

Chapter 12
The Justice League

Batman is a jerk
Fund low income school lunches
Be a real hero

Bruce Wayne plays dress up
He could make a real difference
By creating jobs

Superman can't lose
He is Superman damn it
Not pretty good man

The Flash is so fast
He can not brush his own teeth
Or his head will break

I am sure the Flash
Always gets his paper first
Before his neighbor

Chapter 13
Willy Wonka

Once Wily Wonka
Enslaved a population
Set them free Charlie

The Oompa Loompa
Are kept in captivity
Crap if you ask me

Did you really win
When you got a gold ticket
Still nothing is free

Chapter 14
Count Chocula

When Count Chocula
Turns you into a vampire
Chocolate time baby

Cereal villain
Raconteur Fashion Icon
Coming Halloween

The cereal prize
A tradeoff for cavities
And eating sugar

Chapter 15
Shark Week

The most awesome shark
Is the hammerhead because
They do home repairs

Fought with a shark once
But sharks have no emotions
So he did not cry

Other sharks don't like
Great Whites because of the ego
What makes them so great

How I love shark week
Even more now that I know
They make Trump so scared

Chapter 16
The Orange Menace

Trump you paid a whore
To spank you with your own face
On a magazine

Trump compared his whore's
Nose to a beet then eagle
The art of the deal

Trump is president
Someplace somewhere Lincoln sobs
I got shot for this

Chapter 17
Miscellaneous

What do you call a
Turd with a judo black belt
That is a tough shit

Hey Adam Sandler
What the hell happened to you
You were funny once

Is Charles in charge
And if so in charge of what
Or to ask what not

Charles lives downstairs
I think he watches me sleep
Charles is creepy

The 1990s
Were the best decade ever
And you know this man!

Flannel shirts were in
Girls wore combat boots daily
To kick in the pit

Supernatural
Pre Teen Lit is a real thing
No really it is

No TV Contests
For getting a record deal
Star Search does not count

Hungry Hungry Hippos
Send a bad message for hippos
Just eat what you want

No doubt Pulp Fiction
The greatest film ever made
Please listen to Jules

Football commercial
More expensive than the game
Is the time you waste

Is Casper friendly
I don't know he is a ghost
Maybe play it safe

How about Sauron
Wearing a sweet monocle
Pennybags style

The last man on Earth
Will miss life's consequences
But not the drama

That time a centaur
Worked at Blockbuster video
Never did happen

I went back in time
They asked about the future
I said it is bleak

People are stupid
And will accept poor choices
Made on their behalf

Chapter 18
Swayze

To Wong Foo Thank You
You were cool with dudes as chicks
Way back in the day

Swayze the legend
The feather of your mullet
Inspires us all

Swayze sweet Swayze
Your spin kicks define beauty
How we see violence

We must do the lift
Put Baby in the corner
Not on Swayze's watch

Thank you for reading
The book I worked so hard on
A sequel comes next

Made in the USA
Middletown, DE
29 December 2022

20673100R00076